THE POWER OF GPT-4

YOUR IN-DEPTH GUIDE TO THE LIMITLESS POTENTIALS OF AI

BY RICHARD MCDOUGAL

DEDICATION

To all the brilliant minds who have tirelessly contributed to the development of GPT-4, this book is dedicated to you.

Thank you for your tireless efforts in bringing us one step closer to a future where artificial intelligence can help solve some of the world's most pressing challenges.

Contents

INTRODUCTION

Welcome to the world of GPT-4, OpenAI's most recent and complex natural language processing model. The ground-breaking Generative Pre-trained Transformer series, which has revolutionized the fields of artificial intelligence and natural language processing, has released GPT-4, its fourth iteration.

Because to its improved language processing abilities, GPT-4 is poised to alter the way humans interact with machines and open up new possibilities for language-based applications. A new era of intelligent computing, including virtual assistants and automated content creation, is predicted to begin with GPT-4.

GPT-4 is built on the transformer architecture, just like its forerunners, which enables it to handle text at a level of complexity that was previously impractical. The model can comprehend the context and links between words thanks to the transformer architecture's self-attention capabilities, leading to more accurate and cogent text generation.

The capacity of GPT-4 to produce more text that resembles human speech than any other language model is among its most intriguing qualities. The model will be trained on an unparalleled volume of text data in order to gain a more thorough knowledge of language and human expression.

Also, compared to its predecessors, GPT-4 is able to carry out a greater range of tasks. This includes assignments like translating, summarizing, responding to inquiries, and even original writing.

Concerns exist, nevertheless, regarding the possible effects of such a potent language model. Opponents have expressed concern about the technology's potential abuse, including the generation of increasingly convincing fake news as well as the dissemination of propaganda.

Despite these reservations, GPT-4 is positioned to provide a significant turning point for NLP and AI. It will surely open the door for later language models that are more sophisticated and advanced, with potential uses in a variety of sectors and industries.

PART 1: UNDERSTANDING GPT-4

WHAT IS GPT-4?

Since its release, ChatGPT has seen a number of minor modifications, although none come close to the most recent one: GPT-4. It adds support for image input along with a number of under-the-hood enhancements to the chatbot's capabilities.

Until now, ChatGPT has been built on GPT-3.5, which is a descendant of OpenAI's 2020 language model. Thus, what has changed with GPT-4, and how has this affected your ChatGPT experience?

If you're not already aware of ChatGPT's underlying technology, here's a quick introduction: Generative Pre-trained Transformer is referred to as GPT. It is built on Google's Transformer architecture and was pre-trained on a big collection of text samples. The term "generative" describes the capacity to produce wholly original writing.

As implied by the name, GPT-4 refers to the most recent version of the language model. It replaces GPT-3 and GPT-3.5, the latter of which has operated ChatGPT since its launch in November 2022.

OpenAI released GPT-4, their most recent language model system, on March 14, 2023. The most recent version of the Generative Pre-trained Transformer (GPT) will be available to premium ChatGPT users and through API.

If you feed the GPT-4 a question from a US bar exam, it will write an essay demonstrating legal understanding. It will employ biological expertise if you offer it a medical compound and ask for many alterations.

The ChatGPT chatbot, which was released in November 2022, was powered by GPT 3.5, which served as both its main rival and predecessor.

Text produced by deep learning models known as GPT models has a human-sounding timbre.

HOW DOES GPT-4 WORK?

GPT-4 is powered by a neural network that has amassed a large amount of training data. The model has previously been trained on a big corpus of data, which allows it to understand and produce natural language. After being trained, the model can be adjusted for a specific task, such as language translation, question-answering, or summarizing.

GPT-4 not only generates text that is more accurate and realistic-sounding than its predecessor. It can handle both text and image processing.

The AI is still susceptible to some of the same issues that beset earlier GPT models, such as bias, stepping beyond of the bounds set up to prevent it from saying inappropriate or destructive things, "hallucinating," or confidently creating falsehoods that are not present in its training data.

The most notable difference might be that GPT-4 is "multimodal," or compatible with both text and graphics. It can process and respond to visual inputs, but it cannot create visuals (unlike generative AI models like DALL-E and Stable Diffusion).

Even without its multimodal capability, the new program outperforms its predecessors in tasks that require thinking and problem-solving. Both GPT-3.5 and GPT-4 were put through a variety of human-designed tests administered by OpenAI, including a mock bar exam for attorneys, the SAT and Advanced Placement tests for high school students, the GRE for college graduates, and even a few sommelier exams.

Although GPT-4 consistently outperformed its predecessor, it struggled on tasks involving the English language and literature, scoring at or above human levels on several of these benchmarks. Yet, its extensive problem-solving abilities may be applied to a range of real-world tasks, such as managing a busy schedule, identifying errors in a block of code, explaining grammatical nuances to language learners, and identifying security holes.

More than 25,000 words may be read and output at once by the new model, which can also interpret longer text blocks. Even while older models were employed to create long-form apps, they usually lost their direction. The ability of the new model to produce different genres of artistic output in specific aesthetic forms can be used to characterize its "creativity."

A well-known NLP model is the Generative Pre-trained Transformer (GPT) series. GPT models, which are deep neural networks, train on massive amounts of text input unsupervised. These models can respond to questions, compose essays, and more, among other things

While being less skilled than humans in many real-world situations, the GPT-4 is a substantial multimodal model (accepting image and text inputs and producing text outputs) that performs at a level comparable to people on a range of professional and academic standards.

GPT-4 has enhanced how interdependence, coherence, and common sense thinking are handled. Long-distance relationships between words or phrases in a text are known as long-term dependencies. The logical and consistent way that a text's sentences and paragraphs fit together as a whole is known as its long-range coherence.

Common sense thinking is the process of applying general knowledge or common sense to the outside world in a book. These features of natural language are more effectively captured by GPT-4 than by GPT-3.5, which has a smaller memory capacity, a weaker attention system, and a more limited understanding of semantics.

FEATURES OF GPT-4

- An Enhancement to Language and Code

Generation GPT-4 generates more cohesive, human-like language. GPT-4 shows that code generation has been improved.

- A better understanding of context

It is predicted that GPT-4 will better understand context, making it easier for it to identify the intended meaning of a sentence and offer more correct answers.

- Language Assistance

GPT-4 will support several languages, enabling communication with those who speak various languages easier.

- Support for both text- and image-based input

At the moment, OpenAI only makes the text-based GPT-4 version of the standard available to the public.

- Significance in a longer context

Longer paragraphs are relevant in context (even 50 pages). Versions of 8k (approximately 10–13 pages of text) and 32k (about 50 pages of text) are available using the OpenAI API (when API becomes available).

- A very intriguing aspect of visual interpretation is its multimodality

Along with assisting with picture understanding, GPT-4 gives the image additional context and significance.

HOW IS GPT-4 DIFFERENT FROM GPT-3?

The following are some ways that GPT-4 differs from GPT-3, according to OpenAI:

1. **Capacity and dependability:** Despite not having any particular training, GPT-4 performed among the top 10% of test takers on a simulated exam. GPT-3.5 performed poorly in the same situation, finishing in the bottom 10%.

2. **Image inputs:** Images, graphs, and infographics can be used as inputs in GPT-4 rather than text-based prompts. The use of image inputs in addition to the text is a notable advance. Complex images like charts, memes, and screenshots from academic papers can be handled using GPT-4. Nevertheless, this feature is not yet accessible to the general public and is only currently offered in research previews.

3. **Greater input size:** GPT-4 can accept 25,000 words of input text, allowing it to understand complicated subjects and provide more context in its responses to questions. This is a significant improvement over the current ChatGPT limit of 4,096 characters, which accounts for both the input prompt and the chatbot's reply.

4. **Logical reasoning:** Using logic, GPT-4 reportedly provides 40% more factual responses than its predecessor, according to OpenAI. The model is also less likely to have hallucinations (where it

confidently responds with fake or fictional information).

5. **Creativity:** GPT-4 has more imagination because it can adopt several personas while maintaining character. For instance, it can foretell whether a person would be a tutor or a pirate, the latter of which is illustrated in the screenshot up top. At first glance, these modifications might appear insignificant, yet when taken together, they give GPT-4 a tremendous amount of power.

6. **Lower error rates:** GPT-4 was created to improve model "alignment" by strengthening its comprehension of user intents while generating more precise and offensive output. GPT-4 outperforms GPT-3.5 in terms of factual accuracy and fewer error rates.

7. **Improved Steerability:** Additionally, it enhances "steerability," enabling users to change the model's tone and appearance to suit their preferences. In addition, GPT-4 follows guardrails more closely than its predecessor while rejecting improper requests.

Consider the greater input size as an illustration. You can send GPT-4 a link to any page on Wikipedia and make further inquiries in response. This is crucial for specialized subjects that ChatGPT is probably not very knowledgeable about; after all, we know that it understands only a small portion of many philosophical and scientific ideas.

Moreover, you might ask ChatGPT to generate code snippets by feeding it the documentation for a particular programming language or library. The options are essentially limitless.

BENEFITS OF GPT 4

- **Setting the Scene with Specifics**

An article can be summarised by copying it, pasting it into ChatGPT, and telling it to "Summarize the text into a phrase where every word begins with "G"." When a tutorial on using ChatGPT-3.5 was given, of course, ChatGPT-3.5 failed the evaluation. Nonetheless, GPT-4 can produce the user's request.

GPT-4 can precisely produce the user's desired results by receiving instructions for the assistant to follow.

- **Merging Ideas**

Additionally, GPT-4 permits flexible concept fusion using a variety of articles. By copying and pasting your articles, you can use the ChatGPT-4 help to ask questions like, "Find a topic that unites these two articles."

If the output from the ChatGPT-4 helper wasn't exactly what you were searching for or wasn't insightful enough, you may help it by providing input.

- **GPT-4 construction and generation**

GPT-4 can also be used to build stuff! You will need to supply the assistant with a prompt and a little bit of detail for it to give you exactly what you need. For example, create a Discord bot for me.

Based on the role you assigned ChatGPT-4 in the systems section, the assistant would be assigned as an AI programming aid if you requested something that was code-generated, for example. By doing so, the assistant will be able to produce your request and the prompt.

The assistant's developed code block can be tested to see if it works. If you do make a mistake, just tell the support staff what happened and they'll send you the appropriate code block. You can carry on doing this and instruct the assistant until your code is successful.

- **Mathematical calculations**

Problems involving complex calculations and high-level computations, such as taxes, can be challenging to solve. Currently, ChatGPT-4 can help you with these calculations. For instance, you must identify the ChatGPT-4 system as a TaxGPT so that it is aware of its responsibilities if you require it to calculate a tax problem.

After you provide some background information regarding your problem, the aid will be able to perform mathematical calculations. It's noteworthy to note that the model is not linked to a calculator.

- **Visuals**

The public cannot presently use the image function, but it is being developed! You can ask the helper questions regarding an image that you've entered. While OpenAI is working to improve the model faster, it does currently take a while to produce.

- **Handwriting**

You can photograph some handwritten writing, and ChatGPT can interpret it and convert it to text. Even jokes about how it can recognize doctors' handwriting, which we have all had trouble reading in the past and the present, are being made by certain individuals.

- **Using Materials After September 2021**

As is well known, ChatGPT is unaware of any events that will take place after September 2021. However, you can use ChatGPT to pose your inquiry by providing the information or article as a starting point. The assistant will utilize it as a learning tool to provide you with accurate results.

PART 2: GPT-4 DEVELOPMENT AND ADVANCEMENTS

DEEP LEARNING AND NATURAL LANGUAGE PROCESSING ADVANCES

Strong algorithms and the availability of enormous amounts of data have contributed to recent developments in deep learning and natural language processing. These advancements have allowed for the creation of language models like GPT-4, which can generate human-like text, react to questions, and perform tasks that were previously thought to be beyond the scope of AI.

Many important advancements in deep learning and NLP include:

- **Techniques utilized before training:** Unsupervised learning, transfer learning, and self-supervised learning have all been used to successfully teach natural language processing. These strategies have improved performance on a variety of NLP tasks because they include training a model on a large amount of data before optimizing it for a specific goal.

- **Transformer Models:** This have become the de facto framework for issues with natural language processing since their introduction in 2017. These models can scan extensive text sequences and learn sophisticated word and phrase associations, making them ideal for language modeling.

- **Language Generation:** New advances in language generation have made it feasible to create more intricate models that can create text of a high caliber, such as responses to prompts in natural language, stories, and even poetry.

- **Multi-Lingual Models:** The use of multi-lingual models, which can simultaneously process and create text in multiple languages, has increased. Interlingual communication is improved.

GPT-4 AND MACHINE LEARNING

One example of how machine learning is advancing AI is the GPT-4. Machine learning algorithms are necessary for AI systems to learn from data and improve over time.

Concerning GPT-4, the model has already undergone pre-training utilizing massive amounts of text data, which has allowed it to comprehend the basic linguistic structures and patterns.

20

Yet, machine learning is not just about pre-training models. It also entails modifying them for certain tasks and needs. A range of linguistic tasks, including the creation of chatbots, text summarization, and language translation, can be adapted for GPT-4.

The next development in AI and general natural language processing is GPT-4. Because of its complex language-producing abilities and successful few-shot learning capabilities, GPT-4 has the potential to revolutionize how we communicate with machines and one another. It's exciting to be involved in AI right now, and I can't wait to see what the future brings.

One use for GPT-4 is the analysis of natural language. Natural language processing is the process of instructing computers to understand and translate the human language. The intricacy and depth of human language make it difficult for computers to understand, making this a highly difficult task.

But with GPT-4 and other cutting-edge machine learning algorithms, it may be possible to create machines that can understand and interpret human language.

This might have far-reaching effects in fields like customer service, where chatbots and other automated systems may be trained to understand and respond to user inquiries more naturally and effectively.

Some people worry that these algorithms could become too powerful and be used to manipulate individuals or automate duties that should be carried out by humans.

Yet, the development of technology in the future will be significantly influenced by GPT-4 and other cutting-edge machine learning algorithms. The way we live, work, and engage with the outside world may change significantly as these tools become more potent and are utilized more frequently.

PART 3: USING GPT-4

GETTING STARTED WITH GPT-4

The only components of the new LLM that can be tested in ChatGPT are the text-based ones. By restricting access to GPT-4 to ChatGPT Plus subscribers only, OpenAI made the right choice. This suggests that to access the most latest OpenAI model, you must pay $20 per month.

Steps To Accessing GPT-4

1. Log into your current account on the ChatGPT website. If you don't have an account currently, make one right away.

2. The "Upgrade to Plus" option will be there in the bottom left corner after you've logged in. Just click it.

3. In the pop-up window that appears, select ChatGPT Plus by clicking the green "Upgrade plan" button. The new features of GPT-4 are available to you first through ChatGPT, as was already indicated.

4. Your billing address and payment information must be entered in the following page's right pane.

5. After entering the required data, click the "Subscribe" button. Your ChatGPT+ registration will be complete after your payment has been received and processed. Both the more recent GPT-4 model and earlier AI iterations have become user-friendly.

6. Choose "GPT-4" from the drop-down menu on your screen to get going. You can now communicate with the more knowledgeable and responsive ChatGPT chatbot powered by GPT-4 by putting your questions into the text box in the right pane.

PART 4: IMPLEMENTING GPT-4 IN YOUR BUSINESS

Businesses all around the world are preparing to take advantage of the most recent developments in AI technology with the release of OpenAI's GPT-4 (Generative Pre-Trained Transformer 4).

Several firms are eager to benefit from GPT-4's advances because it is expected to be faster, more precise, and more powerful than its forerunners.

Nonetheless, integrating GPT-4 into your company's procedures calls for thorough planning and preparation. You'll see some advice and techniques here for getting your company ready for GPT-4.

- **Consider Your Company Goals and Use Cases**

Understanding how AI can support the accomplishment of your corporate goals is the first step in becoming ready for GPT-4.

Big language models, like GPT-4, are effective tools that may be applied to a variety of commercial applications, but you must be fully aware of how to use them to meet your unique objectives.

Before implementing GPT-4 into your company's workflows, consider what current projects or procedures could benefit from a little assistance from this flexible NLP model.

Let's take the scenario where you are the manager of a marketing group that focuses on content development. In this scenario, producing interesting material at scale with excellent quality could be a real commercial goal for GPT-4.

You may develop content that appeals to your target audience and increases traffic and engagement by utilizing GPT-4 to study and comprehend consumer preferences and trends.

Alternatively, if you own an online store, you may use GPT-4 to raise client satisfaction and experience. You can find frequent problems and pain points that customers encounter when interacting with your company by utilizing GPT-4 to analyze customer feedback and reviews.

Following that, you may utilize this analysis to optimize your website and enhance customer support, which will promote client loyalty and repeat business.

- **Choose the Proper Model**

Businesses will be able to select from a variety of new models, including 8K and 32K context windows, with the release of GPT-4.

To guarantee that you get the most out of the technology, it's crucial to choose the proper model for your unique needs. While choosing a GPT-4 model for your company, take into account variables such as model size, accuracy, and speed.

For specific jobs, the aforementioned e-commerce corporation might employ two distinct tools. A platform that has honed a model for anomaly detection and examines financial transactions for potential fraud will be distinct from an AI model that is optimized for natural language generation and can be used to automatically generate product descriptions using your brand's voice and tone.

- **Develop Your Team (or Find the Right Partner)**

Your staff will need to pick up new techniques and procedures to integrate GPT-4 into your company workflows.

For your staff to use GPT-4 properly and efficiently, you must give them the necessary training and assistance. To assist your workforce in becoming tech-savvy, think about providing workshops or training sessions.

Think about the e-commerce illustration from earlier. AI needs high-quality data to function properly when analyzing massive amounts of consumer feedback from numerous sources, including product evaluations, emails, chat logs, and support tickets.

Make sure your qualitative data is clear, organized, and pertinent to your company's objectives before integrating GPT-4 into your operations. You'll need to either teach your team about data preparation or locate an outside partner like Viable who can do it for you.

- **Begin Modestly and Iterate**

It's crucial to start small and iterate while integrating GPT-4 into your company workflows. Before scaling up, start with a small-scale project to test the technology and improve your operations.

This strategy enables you to spot any problems or difficulties early on and make adjustments as necessary.

Let's imagine, for instance, that you are in charge of customer experience and that you want to use GPT-4 to automate responses to support ticket inquiries.

You may start by implementing GPT-4 for just one channel, like email, and tracking the precision of the answers. From there, you can gradually add other channels, like chat or social media, and improve your responses in response to client input.

- **Make Sure It's Ethical**

Finally, employing GPT-4 comes with ethical considerations, just like using any other AI technique. It's crucial to make sure you're using technology ethically and responsibly.

When integrating GPT-4 into your operations, take into account elements like bias, privacy, and transparency, and make sure you have policies and procedures in place to resolve any ethical issues.

It takes significant planning, thought, and preparation to integrate GPT-4 into your company workflows. Understanding your business goals and GPT-4 use cases is essential for making the most of the technology and achieving your goals.

You may use GPT-4 to promote growth and innovation by being aware of your needs, picking the ideal model, educating your team, starting small, and iterating.

THE GPT-4'S EFFECTS ON TRADITIONAL INDUSTRIES

Due to GPT-4's extraordinary capabilities, a variety of conventional sectors could be disrupted:

- **Automation:** GPT-4 has the ability to automate a variety of time-consuming operations, including report writing, content creation, and customer service. Businesses will benefit from greater efficiency and cost reductions as a result of this.

- **Making Decisions:** GPT-4 can analyze enormous volumes of data and offer insights that aid enterprises in making wise choices. Particularly advantageous situations can arise in the financial and medical sectors.

- **Personalization:** GPT-4 is capable of producing personalized content that is catered to specific preferences, improving user experiences in a variety of industries, including e-commerce and entertainment.

With the development of prototypes, design concepts, and even software code, GPT-4 has the ability to stimulate the development of new goods and services.

This may result in the development of novel solutions in a variety of sectors, including industry and education. With its image input, the GT-4 can support classification technologies like hazard identification.

PART 5: LIMITATIONS AND CHALLENGES OF GPT-4

EXPLORING THE GPT-4 TRAINING PROBLEMS FOR OPENAI

One of the most potent language models ever developed is OpenAI's GPT-4, which is the most recent iteration of their Generative Pre-trained Transformer. GPT-4 has the potential to completely change how we interact with computers thanks to its outstanding natural language processing capabilities. Yet, there are particular difficulties in training this model.

The magnitude of GPT-4 is one of the main obstacles. The largest model yet released by OpenAI, GPT-4 has over 175 billion parameters. This indicates that the model's training demands a significant amount of data and computational power.

It is not possible to train GPT-4 on a single machine, hence OpenAI has created a distributed training framework that enables numerous machines to cooperate to train the model.

The enormous amount of data required to train GPT-4 presents another difficulty. According to OpenAI's estimation, GPT-4 training needs at least 45TB of data.

To guarantee that the model can produce text with accuracy, this data needs to be carefully curated. A method for gathering and curating data for GPT-4 has been created by OpenAI, however, it is time- and money-consuming.

Last but not least, the GPT-4 model is intricate and needs careful tuning to function as intended. Although OpenAI has created a collection of tools to aid in this process, it is still a challenging and time-consuming task.

Despite these difficulties, OpenAI has achieved considerable advancements in GPT-4 training. The model is now available for usage in numerous applications, such as text production, question-answering, and natural language processing.

GPT-4 has the potential to completely change the way we interact with computers with more study and development.

EXAMINING THE GPT-4 LIMITS OF OPENAI

The GPT-4 language model from OpenAI can completely transform natural language processing (NLP). It is not without its restrictions, though.

GPT-4 has some major flaws, one of which is a lack of contextual awareness. Despite having been trained on a lot of text data, GPT-4 is unable to comprehend the context of the text.

This means that while it is capable of producing meaningful statements, they might not always make sense in the context of a discussion.

GPT-4's dependency on big datasets is another drawback. Even though GPT-4 can produce text from tiny datasets, its performance is not as good as when it is trained on bigger datasets.

This means that GPT-4 is not appropriate for tasks like sentiment analysis or summarization that need a more in-depth comprehension of language.

Ultimately, GPT-4 has a limited capacity to produce original or creative content. GPT-4 cannot produce original thoughts or concepts because it was trained on already-existing text data.

This means that creative or innovative jobs like writing stories or creating artwork are not appropriate for GPT-4.

Overall, the GPT-4 language model from OpenAI is a potent tool with a wide range of potential uses. To ensure that it is utilized properly, it is crucial to be aware of its limitations.

PART 6: APPLICATIONS OF GPT-4

EXAMINING THE POSSIBLE USES OF OPENAL'S GPT-4

The natural language processing (NLP) model GPT-4 from OpenAI can completely alter a variety of industries. GPT-4 is a potent text-generation model that requires little training and can produce text that resembles that of a human. It is the most recent language model that OpenAI has created, and it was trained using a huge dataset of 45 TB of text.

GPT-4 has the potential to be applied in numerous fields, including automated journalism and customer service. GPT-4 could be used in customer service to offer tailored solutions to client inquiries, saving firms time and money.

GPT-4 could be used in automated journalism to produce news articles, freeing up journalists to concentrate on more in-depth reporting.

Moreover, GPT-4 might be used to enhance search engine outcomes. GPT-4 might deliver more precise and pertinent search results by comprehending natural language inquiries. GPT-4 can also be used to create text summaries, which help readers quickly grasp the essential ideas of a document.

GPT-4 could potentially be used to generate text for artistic purposes like song lyrics and poetry. GPT-4 may produce imaginative and emotive prose by comprehending the context of a given prompt.

GPT-4 could be employed to provide natural language responses for virtual assistants like Siri and Alexa. GPT-4 could offer more logical and precise solutions by comprehending the context of a user's question.

TEN WAYS YOU CAN EASILY APPLY GPT-4

1. GPT-4 enables the creation of web applications from simple sketches on napkins

Any drawing a user does on paper or a napkin might act as an idea for a website. After capturing a screenshot of that image and sending it to the AI for evaluation, a functioning website is produced.

The user interacts with a neural network that has been fed a lot of content and trained to predict the outcome, which is how this works. Any data that GPT-4 has gathered from the image is converted into a computer language, such as HTML or JavaScript.

2. It might hasten the creation of playable video games.

GPT-4 can generate working code that can be used to create a video game in a matter of seconds. GPT-4 promptly created a straightforward example utilizing JavaScript and the HTML5 Canvas API when a user asked the chatbot to construct a code block for a game like a ping pong.

The code generated by GPT-4, in contrast to past iterations of GPT, performed flawlessly and without the need for any troubleshooting.

3. GPT-4 can successfully complete and exhibit human-level competency in nearly every exam with some decent scores.

The most recent version, GPT-4, performed very well on a number of standardized academic assessments, including the LSAT, GRE, SAT, and BAR exams.

With a score of 298/400 on the Unified BAR exam, an LSAT score in the 88th percentile, and so forth, it excelled on these tests. It scored highly on AP tests in macroeconomics, microeconomics, US history, and chemistry as well.

4. You don't need any prior coding experience to create a useful Chrome extension.

A step-by-step procedure for creating a Google Chrome extension can be described using GPT-4. GPT-4 mentioned the steps and the source code when asked for an easy pirate-themed extension using manifest version 3.

The purpose of the extension was to read any highlighted content on a webpage, summarize it in "pirate talk," and include a joke with a pirate theme in the open Chrome window.

5. GPT-4 can assist in contextualizing and elucidating the idea behind an image.

When given an image, GPT-4 can understand it and describe what's happening in the background. Even the humor and the purpose are well-stated.

GPT-4 clearly understood an internet meme that ridiculed the state of computer vision and artificial intelligence, and it even explained its humor.

6. GPT-4 can be used to handle legal matters.

DoNotPay, a chatbot for legal services, performs remarkably well on GPT-4 and can generate "one-click lawsuits" for $1,500 worth of robocall cases. One can quickly create a lawsuit of 1000 words that contains a transcription of the call after receiving a call by clicking a button.

7. GPT-4 is useful for assisting parents in their day-to-day activities.

Milo, a sort of GPT-4-powered virtual co-parent for parents, can be used by parents everywhere to do things like add children's birthdays to the calendar, send invitations to birthday parties, make personalized reminders for paying nannies, and more.

It even fixes issues with school newsletters, family whiteboards, and football emails.

8. The newest GPT-4-powered Bing is capable of answering complex inquiries.

Bing can respond to even complex, customized inquiries. It can prepare a three-course meal, produce excellent rhyming poetry, help the user organize an anniversary or fishing trip, create a custom diet plan, etc.

9. The recently introduced Duolingo, which uses GPT-4 as its core technology, makes learning a language quick and easy.

Several new features in the educational technology application Duolingo allow users to learn languages more quickly.

The recently announced Duolingo Max can help users role-play activities like ordering coffee or making trip plans by giving them personalized feedback based on AI in their classes.

10. GPT-4-powered chatbot can be used to explain difficult concepts.

GPT-4 has been adjusted for the Khan Academy learning environment, which is used by students from all over the world and provides some top-notch online learning materials.

Even complex questions can be answered by the chatbot, along with an explanation of its reasoning. A prime example of this is its ability to analyze complex mathematical equations with the necessary logic and solve them methodically.

APPLICATION CASES FOR AI IN AUTOMATION AND DATA INTEGRATION

In the following instances, LLMs can make data and application integrations simpler:

1. Extraction

Business data is primarily stored in SQL-based databases and cloud data warehouses. At least one SQL Snap is present in the pipelines of 65% of our clients.

Writing the queries for these Snaps can be difficult because it requires a thorough understanding of both SQL and the target databases' structures and subtleties unique to each data store. The creation of SQL queries can be made simpler by GPT-4's sophisticated NLP capabilities.

GPT-4 can assist users in creating more precise and productive searches using natural language prompts since it has the capacity to comprehend complicated data structures and relationships. The time and technological know-how needed to extract data from multiple sources can be greatly reduced in this way.

2. Building A Data Pipeline

GPT-4 has the capacity to streamline the development of data pipelines by directing users through the procedure using natural language prompts. Users can reduce manual intervention by expressing their requirements in conversational language, as GPT-4 generates the pipeline's necessary processing flow, expressions, or scripts.

This can help firms create pipelines more quickly and with fewer mistakes. Additionally, GPT-4 can recommend the best data connection configurations, removing the difficulty of connecting to enterprise data.

3. Transformation

GPT-4 assists in streamlining the data preparation process by automating the conversion of data from one format to another.

With the aid of its sophisticated machine learning capabilities, GPT-4 can produce the logic required to automatically transform the data into the correct format by locating patterns and correlations within the data. This can considerably reduce the time and effort needed to prepare the data while also increasing its correctness.

4. Quality control

GPT-4 can assist in orchestrating procedures for data and app integration testing and quality assurance. We have discovered that GPT-4 can summarise small samples of data sets and spot problems with data quality, such as inconsistencies and errors.

Once data cleaning transformations have been applied to a bigger data set using these results, high-quality data will be produced for the target database or cloud data warehouse.

5. Problem-solving

GPT-4 can assist in problem-solving in the event that there are any problems or errors with the data and app integration and orchestration processes. GPT-4 can quickly pinpoint the underlying cause of an issue and make suggestions for potential fixes thanks to its capacity to condense complex data structures and relationships into simple terms as well as to translate complex system error signals into plain language.

This can boost the effectiveness of the system and considerably cut down on the time and effort needed for troubleshooting.

6. Thoughts

Through the use of natural language queries, powerful NLP capabilities in GPT-4 enable users to acquire insights into a portion of company data.

The accuracy of the insights can be improved and the time and effort needed for data analysis can be greatly decreased when non-technical subject matter experts are able to ask inquiries in their own words.

PART 7: ETHICS OF GPT-4

ETHICAL CONSIDERATIONS FOR GPT-4

Tech sector professionals have expressed ethical concerns over OpenAI's GPT-4, a text-generating AI system. The system has received accolades for its potential to transform natural language processing since it can produce text that is similar to that of a human being on any given subject.

However, some experts have cautioned that the technology might be exploited to provide false information and propaganda that is deceptive and misleading.

The GPT-4's ethical ramifications are especially troubling in the context of internet communication. The algorithm can produce language that can pass for human-written content, making it possible to propagate misleading information or sway public opinion.

Also, because the system can produce text on any subject, it might be used to produce false reviews or other types of fraudulent advertising.

Concerns regarding the possibility of GPT-4 being used to produce offensive or improper information have also been expressed by experts.

Due to the system's ability to generate text without human input, it may be utilized without the user's knowledge or agreement to produce offensive or inappropriate information. Users might therefore be exposed to things they otherwise would not have seen or heard about as a result of this.

Finally, academics have expressed worries about the possibility of using GPT-4 to produce discriminatory or prejudiced information.

The system may be used to produce content that reflects the biases of the data because it has been trained on a large number of datasets. This might cause false or biased information to propagate, which could have detrimental effects on society.

Given these moral questions, OpenAI has taken steps to make sure GPT-4 is used ethically. In order to utilize the system, for instance, users must first accept a code of conduct that the corporation has implemented.

In order to prevent the system from producing offensive or improper information, OpenAI has also created a system of checks and balances.

GPT-4 could fundamentally alter natural language processing, but it also poses significant ethical issues. Experts and decision-makers must take into account the potential consequences of the technology's use as it develops and make sure that the necessary safeguards are in place to ensure its responsible use.

CONCLUSION

It is obvious that GPT-4 is a formidable language model with the potential to completely change how humans communicate and interact with technology.

GPT-4 aims to expand AI with its cutting-edge features, which include enhanced machine learning, neural network design, and natural language processing.

GPT-4 has the power to change how we work and live in a variety of fields, including healthcare, banking, customer service, and creative writing.

GPT-4 has the potential to boost productivity, cut expenses, and improve the quality of our lives by automating some processes and enhancing others.

Yet immense power also entails great responsibility. We must be aware of the ethical ramifications of GPT-4 use as we embrace its potential. We must be watchful to make sure that GPT-4 is used in a transparent and accountable manner and does not reinforce prejudice or discrimination.

GPT-4 has undeniable power. Its cutting-edge capabilities have the potential to change how we communicate and engage with technology. But, it is our responsibility to make sure that its usage is morally and responsibly done.

By doing this, we can fully utilize this effective instrument and build a brighter future for everyone.